Re–Entry

Into

Faith

"Courage—be not afraid!"

by Catherine Doherty

Madonna House Publications

Combermere, Ontario, Canada

Madonna House Publications®
2888 Dafoe Rd, RR 2
Combermere ON K0J 1L0

www.madonnahouse.org/publications

Phone: (613) 756-3728
Email: publications@madonnahouse.org

For more information about the Servant of God Catherine
Doherty and her cause, see:

www.catherinedoherty.org

Re-Entry Into Faith by Catherine de Hueck Doherty
© 2012 Madonna House Publications. All rights reserved.

Cover Art: Helen Hodson "Peter coming to Jesus through a
storm"

Unless otherwise noted, Scripture quotations are taken from
the Jerusalem Bible, copyright © 1966 Darton, Longman &
Todd, London, and Doubleday & Company, Inc., New York.

Library and Archives Canada Cataloguing in Publication

Doherty, Catherine de Hueck, 1896-1985

Re-entry into faith : "courage—be not afraid! " / Catherine de Hueck Doherty.

ISBN 978-1-897145-34-0

1. Faith. I. Title.

BT771.2.D643 2012   234'.23   C2012-901997-6

Dedicated to Father Gene Cullinane (1907-1997)

Pioneer priest of Madonna House Apostolate

Man of strong faith

Why should I want to do this? Faith, my friends, faith! Simple, unadulterated, idiotic, superb, beautiful, enticing, holding up, lifting up, pulling down, full of challenge, full of crises, full of excitement, alive faith!

Catherine Doherty

Table of Contents

About the Author 6

Part I

God's Gift to Us 13
You Are Loved 16
Prostrate Before Him 20
Portal to Faith 23
To Believe and To Love 26
Mother in Faith 29

Part II

The Mercy of God 35
The Mystery of "Uselessness" 37
Face to Face 40
God's Will—True Life 43
Courage to Witness 47
Temptations Against Faith 49

Part III

Faith and Self-acceptance 55
Show Your Faith 59
Faith in a Child 62
A Living Faith 64

Part IV

A Loving Hand in Trials 69
Love Your Enemies 73
The Ordinary is Sacred 77
The Keys of Faith 80
Jesus Is Here 84
Fiat – Yes 85
Martyrdom and Death 89

About the Author

Catherine Doherty's long life spanned most of the 20th century. Born in Russia in 1896 and falling asleep in the Lord in Canada in 1985, she personally experienced and suffered through many of the cataclysmic events of that century. The Holy Spirit used these events, and her experiences and suffering, to communicate graces to her for the enrichment of the whole Church.

Catherine was born and raised in a wealthy and deeply Christian family. She served as a nurse with the Russian Army in the First World War, but after the Communist Revolution was forced to flee her homeland—she and her husband and son immigrated to Canada as refugees. For some time she worked at menial jobs to provide for her family, which gave her an experience of poverty, but also, as she would later say, deepened her faith and dependence on God.

Through a chance meeting, her talent as a public speaker was discovered, and in the 1920s she was a successful lecturer throughout North America, speaking about her life in Russia and her experience of the Revolution. Her marriage was disintegrating, however, and later was annulled.

Living in comfort again with the success of her lecturing, Catherine found herself pursued by Christ's words, "Sell all you possess, and come follow Me." This was the time of the Great Depression, and with the blessing of the Archbishop of Toronto, Catherine gave away her possessions and went to live a life of prayer and simple service to the poor in the slums of Toronto. Others came to join her, and the work developed into an apostolate she called Friendship House, which provided food, clothing, and spiritual support to those in need.

Because her approach was so different from what was being done at the time, she encountered resistance, and Friendship House closed in Canada. Soon Catherine was invited to open another in New York City's Harlem. Catherine was horrified by the injustices she saw done to black people, and she used her speaking gifts to travel the country decrying racial discrimination—in this she was a forerunner of the movement for civil rights in the U.S. The Great Depression was followed by World War II. Although Catherine remained in North America, she was aware of the suffering of her own mother and siblings in war-torn Europe.

Again due to misunderstandings, Catherine was forced to leave Friendship House. In 1947 she returned to Canada, to the village of Combermere, with her second husband, newspaperman Eddie Doherty. What seemed like the end of the road turned out to be the most fruitful period of Catherine's life. Her example of radical Gospel living became a magnet for men and women in search of a way to live their faith. The community of Madonna House was born, and has grown into a family of lay men, lay women, and priests, living under promises of poverty, chastity, and obedience.

Catherine sensed and witnessed the de-Christianization of the Western world as the 20th century unfolded, and over time exemplified and communicated a faith vision for the restoration of the Church and our modern culture. The Madonna House training center in Combermere offers an experience of this Gospel life to guests who come—they participate fully in the daily life of the community. In this Madonna House way of life are the seeds of a new Christian civilization.[1]

During the many years of her apostolic life, Catherine's voice and her pen spoke out. In

---

1   For further information about Madonna House see our website at www.madonnahouse.org

lectures and talks up and down the North American continent, and in a ceaselessly flowing river of articles, letters, and books, she penetrated the lives of Christians with the unwavering message of the need to live the Gospel. She insisted that the core of the Good News is God's love for us.

Catherine's faith was greatly challenged in her experience of some of the most significant events of the 20th century. As she lived through them, her faith and her love grew stronger and more mature. As a wife and mother, writer and lecturer, as one whose experience and gifts could form a whole community of men and women, she was involved in the myriad facets of existence. God taught her much wisdom through her long life, and she grew ever closer to him. The intensity of her union with God could shatter the mediocrity of those who encountered her, and many people who met or heard her speak only once found their lives radically changed by that single, powerful, and charismatic encounter.

The depth of her spiritual legacy stems both from her personal gifts, and from the extraordinary range of experiences through which God finely honed and forged them.

She serves as a sure guide for others in the life of faith.

Part I

*I live in faith ... in the Son of God
who loved me
and sacrificed himself for my sake.*

Gal 2:20

We must not forget that very many people, while not claiming to have the gift of faith, are nevertheless sincerely searching for the ultimate meaning and definitive truth of their lives. This search guides people onto the path that leads to the mystery of God. Human reason, in fact, bears within itself a permanent summons, indelibly written into the human heart, to set out to find the One whom we would not be seeking had He not already set out to meet us.

Pope Benedict XVI: *Porta Fidei*, Para.10

God's Gift to Us

Doing the works of God is this:
believing in the One whom he has sent.

Jn 6:29

The other day I was sitting with a priest who came to visit me on my island. It was one of those beautiful, cold, sunny days that Canada is so celebrated for. The river was a sheer, lovely blanket of snow, tinted pink by the setting sun. I think that Russians and nature automatically go together. We live in its symbols and its delights.

The priest was talking about faith. Strangely enough, I had been meditating on faith for quite awhile. It seemed that faith wanted to clarify itself for me so that I might clarify it for others.

The priest said to me, "Catherine, people often believe faith to be a set of moral obligations. Many lay people, clergy and religious see it this way. Oh, yes, we believe, but it is mostly with the head that we believe."

I looked at the snowy expanse of the river, now tinged with the blue shadows of the evening and cried out, "But that's not faith!"

Faith is a gift, a gift given by God to man. We receive the Christian faith through Baptism, when we are immersed in the death and resurrection of Jesus Christ. As we grow into adulthood, faith is assented to again and again. It is the *fiat* or *yes* of one who, as he grows to maturity, continues to say, "I believe."

Faith is a country of darkness into which we venture because we love and believe in the Beloved, who is beyond all reasoning, all understanding, all comprehension. And at the same time, paradoxically, is enclosed within us: the Father, the Son, and the Holy Spirit. Faith must go through this strange dark land, following him whom it loves.

Christ, our Beloved, becomes the door, the way into and through this darkness. And suddenly our heart knows that if we will pass through the door and walk along that way, we will see the Father.

What does it mean to see the Father? It means to assuage that hunger that has been put in man's heart by God himself, the hunger of finally meeting absolute love. We yearn for it. All of us do. We arise and go on a pilgrimage, guided only by faith that we must journey toward the face of perfect Love—because for this we were created, to be one with that Love.

If we embark upon this quest, into the land where we may not be able to hear, may not be able to see, may not be able even to speak, suddenly we will be mysteriously visited. A hand will touch our ears and they will be opened, not only to the speech of man but to the speech of God. A hand will touch our eyes and we will see, not only with our eyes, but with the sight of God. A hand will touch our tongue, and we will speak, not only as men do, but as God speaks, and we will become prophets of the Lord.

True, on the road to the Father we shall fall, for we shall sin. We may turn away from God, we may leave the Church, we may think that we have left everything. But faith being a gift of God, it does not desert us; we desert it, but it follows us. We leave the Church, but the Church—which is part of faith, for it is part of Christ—does not leave us. We turn away from God, but God never turns away from us.

You Are Loved

I am the good shepherd:
the good shepherd is one
who lays down his life for his sheep.

Jn 10:11

When I was a young wife in Petrograd, the city was in chaos as the communists took over. My husband Boris and I were sleeping on the floor after everything was taken away from us. I said to him, "Boris, I am afraid." He yawned and said, "Why? You are a Christian." That was a pretty good answer; I never forgot it. If I am a Christian, can I give way to hopelessness? No. The resurrected Christ is in our midst.

What we have to battle in this day and age is our own hopelessness. Many people are depressed. They are depressed by the image of themselves. They don't think they're doing much. Well, the picture they see in the mirror is cockeyed.

Then, on top of this depression, and in it and over it, comes a terrible loneliness. This applies to lay people, to priests, to everyone. The answer to it is so utterly simple, almost childlike. The answer is faith. A very small word, but one of such immense power that it can lift you to the very feet of God. Faith in who you are, what you stand for, where you are going.

These days, who of us does not need faith, love, peace, compassion, understanding? Especially since many people cannot escape from their fears that bay like a pack of wolves at their heels. They are fearful of everyone in authority, frightened of themselves, filled with inferiority that they should not exist.

Let us stop listening to these nonsensical fears. We don't have to worry about our sinfulness. Forget all this nonsense about being ugly and unlovable. Throw yourself into the arms of God who incarnated himself to become like you and me.

Faith tells you that you are loved by God. Without it, you go down into the pit of your own hell. The wrong self-image puts you right into this pit. When you think of your own image, stop! Look in a mirror and repeat the words from Genesis, "and God saw all he had made and it was very good" (Gn 1:31).

When you have an inferiority complex—and who of us hasn't—you say things like, "I just don't believe that what God made is good. Look at me, I'm a louse." Don't dare to challenge God like this. Everything he made is good, including yourself. Don't listen to that serpent who is giving you apples that look red on the outside and are full of inferiority complexes on the inside. Don't eat that apple, or else you are going to go down into a pit prepared by Satan for you for your whole life.

How can you have a wrong image of something or someone that God touched? God touched you and he created you. You passed through his mind and you were begotten. Anyone of us that passes through God's mind, anyone of us that God touched, cannot be this horrible person we think we are. No! Each one of us is beautiful—we're beautiful because he touched us.

Sometimes this is very difficult for us to accept. We look at ourselves and say, "He made us in his image, equal to himself in a manner of speaking, heir to his Son? This just can't be. He hasn't looked into my heart. He doesn't know what I'm made of!" We say those silly things because our evaluation of ourselves is very poor. We haven't looked at ourselves with the merciful, tender, compassionate eyes of God. So we walk in despair half the time. As a result, the ability to realize that God is both in our midst and in us—a realization that is the fruit of faith—fades and disappears.

This is the main reason, it seems to me, why the Father sent his Son to us, why the Word was made flesh and dwelt amongst us as one of us. The Father, having given us the fantastic gift of faith, wanted to help us accept this awesome gift. He sent his Son Jesus Christ so that we, unbelieving, might believe. We are like children; we need to touch.

Every human being is a mystery. The mystery of man enters into the mystery of God, and bursting forth with great joy, comes faith and understanding. When faith is there, all is clear, and a love relation with God enters into your heart. When you have faith, it is such a simple thing to accept his love, even if you do not understand why he loves you.

Prostrate Before Him

Blessed are the poor in spirit.

Mt 5:3

The only way to approach faith is on our knees, through prayer. We should not only kneel but be prostrate before him, falling on our faces, imploring, crying out for growth in faith, so that we may believe ever more firmly, not only in God but also in one another—we who are fashioned in God's image.

Yes, we can reach God very simply when we prostrate ourselves before him. When I come before God like this I am transformed. And I need to be transformed.

Here I am, an arrogant and proud human being, capable of walking on the moon, of making fantastic instruments that send us pictures of other planets. In my arrogance and pride I am once again polishing the apple to eat, so to speak, to prove I am equal to God.

Suddenly, I realize my works are but nothing. God is God, and I am not. I am his creature, the poor man of the Lord, the poor man of the Beatitudes. I realize that he really meant what he said: "Without me you can do nothing" (Jn 15:5).

Prostration is humility. It's an acknowledgement of who I am, and who he is. A "prostrated Church" is a Church of what I call the *humiliati*: the poor, the forgotten, the lonely. It includes the widow who put her last two cents into the temple collection, and the prostitute, and the thief.

The *humiliati* is the working-class mother who doesn't know how to get her money together—there's not enough of it to feed and clothe everybody. All those who sorrow, all those who seek, all are turning their faces to God. All these enter into faith. All are prostrated before God. All experience God.

It is inconceivable that we shall reach God through books. We shall reach God as he reached us, by covering our brokenness with his incarnation. By incarnating himself, he has made us divine. We partake of this incarnation through prayer and through the deep silence of the prostrated Church. It is not the silence of passivity, but the silence of fire and flame that possesses any person who approaches the invisible.

Faith grows with each prostration of ours. Faith grows with each acknowledgement within us of the Father, the Son, and the

Holy Spirit—the one in three and three in one—within us.

Only children can talk of mysteries as if they were realities. As we lie prostrate before God we have to cry out in faith, "Lord, give me the heart of a child and the awesome courage to live it out as an adult." Then, when we arise from this strange, humbled position, we, like children, can dare to explain the unexplainable. As the Lord said, "It is to such as these that the kingdom of heaven belongs" (Mt 19:14).

Portal to Faith

As soon as Jesus was baptized
he came up from the water,
and suddenly the heavens opened
and he saw the Spirit of God
descending like a dove
and coming down on him.
And a voice spoke from heaven,
"This is my Son, the Beloved;
my favor rests on him."

Mt 3:16-17

It is strange, but when I talk about faith I hear water. I hear little waves splashing on the sand. Then, quite suddenly and inexplicably I hear footsteps, and I am filled with awe. I know that Christ is approaching to be baptized. Nothing is as profound as the baptism of the Son of God.

Just look and listen. A man stands naked to be baptized, and that man is God. He enters into his creature, which is water, and he is baptized by his creature which is man. He immersed himself in that water so that you and I, and all of us who follow him, could go through the waters of baptism. Faith is given to us in baptism, that we might grow in it. Then, slowly, as a child grows, we enter into the mystery of faith.

In baptism you are joined to the Mystical Body of Christ. When you become part of his body, one of his people, a sheep of his flock, faith whispers to you about the resurrection: "Open your eyes and see. See the dazzling light that comes forth from the East. It is our Lord rising from the dead." As you behold the light of this mystery in the darkness of faith, light and darkness are mingled together, and you can almost faint from what is pouring into your heart. Jesus died for us and rose as he promised so that we might have this faith. I often think that Niagara Falls is a puny little stream compared to the rushing waters of baptism that lift us up to the feet of the Father.

St. Paul says, "When we were baptized in Christ Jesus, we were baptized in his death. In other words, when we were baptized we went into the tomb with him, and joined him in death, so that as Christ was raised from the dead by the Father's glory, we too might live a new life" (Rom 6:2-11). St. Paul visualized baptism by total immersion as is done in the Eastern Church. By immersion, we enter into the death of Christ. In the Roman rite, water is usually poured over the child's forehead, symbolizing this entry into the death of Christ.

St. Paul felt very strongly about this meaning of baptism. It was also understood in this way by the early Christians, and by the Church through the centuries. This is the essence of our life, those of us who believe deeply, who walk in faith. I come together with the death of Christ at my baptism. Something fantastically, incredibly awesome, beyond all imagination, happens to me and in me, in baptism.

Just think for a moment: Father, Son, and Holy Spirit now truly abide in me. God dwells in me. Christ said it: "My Father and I will come and abide in you" (cf. Jn 14:23). The mystery of the Trinity dwells in the mystery of man. I come together with the death of Christ at my baptism. Something encompassed only by faith, not by the intellect, has happened to me and in me.

To Believe and To Love

*"Faith is the assurance
of things not yet seen"*

Heb 11:1

The tragedy of our modern world is that it wants proof that God exists. There is no such proof. No amount of books, libraries, erudite people, or marvelous speakers can convince us that God exists. We enter into the unseen mysteries of our faith, the mystery of God, through an experience, an event, a happening, a miracle.

Once upon a time the second person of the Most Holy Trinity walked this earth. Somewhere there is a spot of land that has kept his footprints. You might not see them but they are there! To make all things clear the Son died for us. Before he died he brought us a new covenant, a new contract if you like. After he died he resurrected! At that moment faith exploded like a thousand stars, or suns, or moons. Love became a platter and presented itself to each of us carrying faith.

This pits our peanut-brain against the mystery of faith. We want to tear apart the very thin veil of faith, to see if we can weigh it, measure it. Faith always eludes us when we approach it this way.

Those of us who have been baptized have received faith as a grace of God, a very special gift. This gift has to be constantly reaffirmed. It is so important to continue to ask for it, to implement it and to act as if I believe. Then the whole of the world is in me and I am in the whole world because God belongs to me and I belong to God.

Through faith we are able to turn our faces to God and meet his gaze. Each day becomes more and more luminous. The veil between God and man becomes less and less until it seems as if we can almost reach out and touch God.

Faith is a pulsating thing; a light, a sun that nothing can dim if it exists in the hearts of men. That's why it's so beautiful. God gives it to me saying, "I love you. Do you love me back? Come and follow me in the darkness. I want to know if you are ready to go into the things that you do not see yet, on faith alone."

Then you look at God, or at what you think is God in your mind, and you say, "Look, this is fine, but you're inviting me to what? An emptiness? A nothingness? There is nothing to see. I cannot touch you. I cannot feel you." Then God goes on to say, "I invite you to a relationship of love: your love of me, my love of you."

Yes, God comes to us as an invitation to love. True, his invitation to love is crucifixion. In a strange and incomprehensible way the pain of the crucifixion that we foresee blends into the joy of an alleluia of his resurrection. As he is crucified, so he is risen. So, too, do we die and rise. No sooner is he taken off the cross and put into the tomb than the stone is rolled back. He is not there. Here is where faith enters. With Mary Magdalene who was the first to see him, we cry "Rabboni! Master!"

At this moment love surges in our heart like a tremendous sea that takes us in and lays us in the arms of God whom we haven't seen but in whom we believe. Across the waves we hear, "Blessed are they who have not seen and yet believe" (Jn 20:29). Now I walk in the darkness of faith and I see. I see more clearly than is possible with my fleshly eyes.

Now I am free because I believe. That's true freedom. Believe without end, believe without frontiers, believe without any kind of proofs, any kind of walls. Just believe.

Mother in Faith

"I am the handmaid of the Lord,"
said Mary,
"let what you have said be done to me."
And the angel left her.

Lk 1:38

I love to meditate on Our Lady. I've written a lot of poems about her. I believe she holds my heart in her hands. I like to think about those hands that embraced all the household tasks: cooking, sweeping, weaving. The hands that embraced God.

Imagine a fourteen or fifteen-year-old girl having an angel stand before her and say, "Hail, full of grace, the Lord is with thee" (Lk 1:28). How does it feel to be addressed by an angel? Strange as it might seem, this woman-child answered regally, simply, directly, without false modesty. She said, "How can this happen to me for I do not know man?" (Lk 1:34) Then she was told that the Holy Spirit would overshadow her. She responded by saying, "Let it be done unto me according to his will" (Lk 1:38). What faith! She simply said yes to the impossible. The strange, incredible, unbelievable faith of a young girl. Faith that gave us God.

Now that's something that should penetrate our hearts. Do you feel it penetrating your heart?

You see, she was a person, a human being just like you and me. Isn't that amazing? True, she had certain graces given her, but she did not understand many things. No, she didn't understand them. She put these things in her heart. She plunged into faith.

This child took a plunge into faith so deep it gives me goose bumps. When you have difficulties in faith, turn to her. She will help you say, "Let it be done according to his will."

Joseph, too, seeing her become large with her Child and, no doubt, seeing the neighbors looking askance, had to trust in the dream he was sent. He, too, plunged into faith. He, too, will hear your prayer.

I bow low before this little girl-woman. She is truly the mother of all those who believe. She had a faith beyond our understanding. I invite you to enter into that solitude of faith that Mary had. Close your mind and open your heart. Enter the solitude of faith. Do not worry about going apart to a quiet place. The solitude of faith is at this very moment, whether you are on a bus or sitting at a table. Do you really believe? All you have to do is what Mary did. Enter the solitude of faith and say yes. That's all.

Part II

*That Christ may live
in your hearts
through faith.*

Eph 3:17

A Christian may never think of belief as a private act. Faith is choosing to stand with the Lord so as to live with Him.

Pope Benedict XVI: *Porta Fidei*, Para. 10

What the world is in particular need of today is the credible witness of people enlightened in mind and heart by the word of the Lord, and capable of opening the hearts and minds of many to the desire for God and for true life, life without end.

Pope Benedict XVI: *Porta Fidei*, Para. 15

The Mercy of God

One of the criminals hanging there …
said, "Jesus, remember me
when you come into your kingdom."
"Indeed, I promise you," he replied,
"today you will be with me in paradise"

Lk 23:39, 42-43

This word to the good thief is a consolation for all who feel guilty because of their sins. Let guilt be wiped out. If any one of you feels guilty and you know that you deserve it, fear not. Look at Jesus Christ. You only need to say, "Have mercy on me." Then, with the eyes of faith that I have tried to tell you about, see an unseen hand wipe out all your sins and misdemeanors. You will realize you are in paradise because he who is merciful dwells in you. Where he is, there is paradise. It is as simple as that.

After confession of sin, guilt should be totally alien to the Christian who has faith. Faith permits us to know the mercy of God. It enables us to read and absorb what God said in torment while he was dying: "Today you will be with me in paradise."

I had a patient in a hospital, and this patient told me that he didn't believe in God at all.

As his sickness progressed he got worse and worse. So he took my hand in his and said, "Nurse, do you believe in God? Do you believe that he is present?" I said, "Yes, I do." He said, "Well, all my life I said he wasn't present. I didn't believe in him. What do you think he will do to me?" I said, "He will embrace you. God understands all things."

Faith assures us that when we come close to God with sorrow in our heart, his consuming fire cleanses everything in us. His arms reach out and take us in and rock us back and forth. We rest against his breast and are lulled by the heartbeats of God.

The Mystery of "Uselessness"

Whoever remains in me,
with me in him,
bears fruit in plenty.

Jn 15: 5

Sometimes, due to sickness or an accident, we find ourselves unable to participate in the normal activities of every day. Then we are greatly tempted to say things like: "Oh, I'm not doing anything! I've been sick for two weeks, a burden on my family, on my community; a burden, period." You can be sure the devil is nearby, rubbing his hands together and saying, "Here I come!" We leave ourselves wide open to him when we do not understand the usefulness of uselessness.

Look at a crucifix. On it is a man, a person like you and me—flesh, muscles, blood—crucified. The nails penetrated his hands and his feet. He was stretched out. People look at this and wonder how useful was he hanging there for three hours? Why didn't he walk around and do a few miracles? That would have been a lot more useful.

This kind of thinking doesn't go with faith. We fail to grasp that by his three hours of suffering the Son of God redeemed the whole world.

Faith convinces us that when we are useless, we are most useful to God. There is such a depth to our usefulness that it shakes me to think about it.

When I was nursing I always told people about it. I said, "Look, here you are, lying immobile with your leg in traction. You're a Christian. You went to Communion. Offer it up. Let this pain go to the world. Take it in your hands like your hands were a chalice. Lift it up. Then you become a most powerful person."

We had a staff worker here who died from cancer. She offered her life for priests and for our apostolate. That was some years ago, and I still get letters from priests who heard about her or who met her for a fleeting instant. It was during the years following Vatican II and many priests were leaving. In the midst of all this uncertainty and confusion and pain, this ordinary woman was lying in bed doing absolutely nothing except telling God she offered him her suffering for priests. A priest wrote, "I had heard about the woman offering herself for priests and she entered into my heart. I stayed in my Order."

Now she didn't meet him, he never came here, so what happened? God happened. God picked up those sufferings and used them. The usefulness of uselessness.

Be on the watch for doubts about this kind of thing. They're natural, they're human, but they're not of faith. Gather up the doubts, the temptations. Make a nice little bundle of them and at night put them at the feet of Our Lady. She will dispose of them as only a mother can. Then you will arise with fewer doubts, and you won't leave yourself open to the promptings of the devil.

Face to Face

Whoever comes to me,
I shall not turn away.

Jn 6: 37

God passionately desires to give us faith. He wants us to ask for it, for only he can give it to us—that is, of course, after his original gift to us in Baptism. He wants us to ask for faith again and again, ask for an increase of it, for a constant increase of it.

When we ask for faith it seems we are, as it were, turning our face toward his face. It seems that God desires this very simple action to happen so that he and we are face-to-face! He wants to look at our face; he loves to see our face facing him. Yet so often we avoid this simple act. Even while we beg him for various favors, we somehow close not only our physical eyes but the eyes of our soul, strangely avoiding looking at him. But we need to remember that he always looks at us, looks at us with deep love.

Faith is that God-given gift that has healed so many who believed in God: the leper, the blind man, the woman with the issue of blood, the servant of the Roman soldier—and millions of others who are not mentioned in the Bible or outside of it.

Faith—the father of love and of hope, as well as of trust and confidence. Faith—that sees God's face in every human face. As it grows and as we pray and beseech God for it, faith identifies us with Christ. Faith heals by asking God to heal. Faith heals others because of the faith I have in the Lord.

Faith walks simply, "childlikely", between the darkness of human life and the hope, the knowledge through faith, of what is to come. "For eye has not seen, nor ear heard what God reserves for those who love him" (cf. 1 Cor 2:9).

Faith—an incredible, fantastic reality, untouchable, unweighable. Faith—contact between God and man. In faith the eyes of God meet the eyes of man, until there is such a little veil between us and the reality that is God, it seems we can almost touch Him.

Faith breaks barriers. Faith makes out of love a bonfire. Faith is contagious when shown by any one of us to the other.

We certainly must pray for faith, especially to preach the Gospel with our lives. Without faith we cannot do it. We must enter into trust and confidence with quiet steps but without hesitation, without cerebration. Truly, here is the moment of the heart, not of the head. The head will rationalize. The head will turn its face away from faith, from love, from hope. The head will put its hand behind its back, so as not to touch the martyr, the prostitute, the publican.

If we have faith in God, we have faith in men. Even the most evil one of us has some redeeming feature, and faith will seek it out. Faith is fundamentally a type of folly, a folly that belongs to God himself.

It is so important to have faith in each other; for it is only through faith that we can communicate. Without faith there is no communication, and there is no love. Without faith, our love will be ill, thin, and tired, and our communication will be just as miserable. Faith alone will restore it.

God's Will—True Life

*What we ask God is that
through perfect wisdom
and spiritual understanding
you should reach
the fullest knowledge of his will.
So you will be able to lead the kind of life
which the Lord expects of you.*

Col 1:9-10

How do we know the will of God? Well, the first thing is to get your own will out of the way. That means you have to pray and you have to have faith.

To enter the total darkness of faith is something that very few people want to do these days. They want to manage themselves. "I can lead my own life. Nobody is going to tell me what to do." That's what the average person feels like. They are in charge of their life. They decide it all.

A very small group says, "Lord, I have received my life from you. You died so that I might live. I throw my life at your feet and sing. It's such a small thing. Now it's yours to do with as you wish."

Many people have looked me straight in the eye and said, "I have not wanted to look at God's will because I was afraid of it." They are afraid that God is going to ask them to do something that they do not wish to do. Well, at that stage, there is no faith.

Faith presumes belief in a person. The person of Jesus Christ who is Love incarnate. The one who came to do the will of his Father. The one who gave up his life for you and me.

You see, you will find the will of God when you stop thinking about your own will. Just "close the wings of your intellect" and enter the darkness of faith.

It's as if you're walking through an absolutely dark night in an unknown country. Your feet are bare and you step very carefully along the path. Your toes are grasping every inch of ground so as not to fall through a crevice. Your hands are outstretched to feel the way. You can't see anything. That's like faith. God has laid out a path for us but he wants us to follow it in darkness. There is fear in entering darkness, but not in the darkness of faith. At the end of the journey there is the Lord waiting for you.

Sometimes this path has fantastic difficulties along it. A man wrote me a letter after he had visited here at Madonna House and said, "Catherine, you lied to me. You told me that God was love and this sort of thing and I arrive home and my mother is dying from cancer. Things are terrible. You're a liar."

Well, I'm not a liar. He hasn't understood what suffering means. Faith, like love, walks hand in hand with suffering. Even though you may be a genius and understand everything, you have to become like a child in order to believe.

We have to throw ourselves at God's feet and say, "Lord, what you are asking is totally impossible!" Then he bends down and picks us up and says, "Child, with me, the impossible takes five minutes more. Come." Now faith, like a lance, goes straight through you. You feel shattered by what you are facing, but you are able to move. You know God will take care of you.

Our Lord died on a cross. You could call it stupidity. I call it the folly of love. He was so in love with you and me that he was willing to die in that fashion with all his intellect perceiving what was going to happen. Faith is like that.

To know the will of God is to enter into that kind of faith and say to God, "*Credo*, I believe! Against all odds, I believe!"

When you believe, when you have faith, wisdom enters. Some call it discernment. With this wisdom you begin to understand the will of God. It becomes clear.

Courage to Witness

When the Advocate comes,
whom I shall send to you
from the Father,
the Spirit of truth…
you too will be witnesses.

Jn 15:26-27

This is the age in which we must transmit and lavishly sow faith into a technological society against all odds, especially intellectual ones. Sow faith into a society demanding that everything be measured, weighed, collated and put into cubbyholes.

In the midst of this, we are called to sow the seeds of faith in the souls of men, for in each there is still left a field, a hill, an old garden that demands re-seeding. But man doesn't want to be put into a cubbyhole; he needs the open spaces to live, to be himself. He especially needs the spiritual "open spaces" for which he hungers. These are the spaces where God dwells, for it is for God he hungers.

This is the age of faith to be given, not only to those who have lost faith, but to those who have wrapped it up and buried it somewhere deep within themselves. So deep that perhaps there are moments when they forget that they ever had it, or where they have hidden it.

It is up to us Christians to show by our lives that God is with us. It is for us Christians to be a light to others' feet, and to put those feet on a path where they will find the faith they think they have lost, but which they have simply put aside. This path is a path of prayer, both for them and for us.

For us, so that we will have the courage to recognize this age of faith that is in *diaspora*, to sow that faith by incarnating it in our lives, by living the Gospel, by praying and by becoming pilgrims of it—pilgrims with an eternal lantern in our hands: the lantern and light of Christ.

Temptations Against Faith

You can trust God
not to let you be tried
beyond your strength,
and with any trial he will give you a
way out of it
and the strength to bear it.

1 Cor 10:13

We say that we believe. And yet do we? At the slightest difficulty, we cry to God, and if he doesn't answer our prayer within the next five minutes or ten, or twenty-four hours, we begin to doubt. We need to get our heart in tune with God's heart.

Because, you see, he's a lover, and he wants us to love him back. For this, he incarnated himself, lived as a man for a number of years, and died a martyr on a cross, all for me. And, by so doing, reconciled me with his Father. I believe that this is so.

When I believe, I am like a tree standing by the water, and I shall not be moved. Yet a tree can be hit by lightning. But for a man or a woman of faith, the lightning passes through them and doesn't touch them, because their faith is strong as God is strong. God doesn't abandon people.

You can say to me, "Well, how do I get that kind of a faith?" On your knees. (Maybe not literally on your knees, although kneeling can be a good position!) You ask for it. The God who has given you faith in Baptism, when you died in Christ and resurrected in Christ, is not going to say "no" to your request. If there is one request that he says "yes" to all the time, always, it's a request to grow in faith.

Now and then we all feel tremors begin to shake our faith. Then we must ask God, implore him, beg him, to give us faith, to increase our faith. We can simply say to him, "Look, Lord, I need this faith, because unless I increase in faith I won't increase in love". Now, wouldn't that be disastrous, not to increase in love? And if my faith is wobbly, and I murmur against God, and so forth, what happens to hope? I need faith so as to have hope.

When doubts come, as come they will because we're human; when mistrust comes, because it will, for we're human, why don't we look this whole thing straight in the face? From where do we have those doubts? From where comes this shakiness? Take, for instance, myself. Seventeen times I've said to God, "I've had it, I can't hack it anymore, it's too much". And seventeen times I've gone into a church—which of course was my undoing, and at the same time the right thing to do—because once I entered a church I understood from whence my temptations came: Satan.

A heart that is in love with God radiates light. One doesn't know this oneself, but others do. But one creature really knows, and that's Satan. When he sees a person from whom light radiates, he comes and attacks through every little chink in that person. He is pretty clever and will use weaknesses of all kinds in order to squash the light—because that light brings people to God. So take a look inside of yourself, and ask yourself, "Is Satan tempting me?"

When pain comes, we cannot help complaining sometimes. Remember that Christ came, and he did something to pain: he made it holy. What is most extraordinary, he made it joyful. That is the whole difference.

Now it all changes and the light grows greater. The devil comes, but he has no chink to enter, because we have understood—by the grace of God and through prayer, in our asking for growth of faith—that temptations are permitted by God; we understand that we should refuse them. Then each one of them becomes a stepping-stone up the mountain of the Lord.

Part III

*What matters is faith
that makes its power
felt through love.*

Gal 5:6b

The "door of faith" (Acts 14:27) is always open for us, ushering us into the life of communion with God. To enter through that door is to set out on a journey that lasts a lifetime. It begins with baptism (cf. Rom 6:4) and it ends with the passage through death to eternal life.

Pope Benedict XVI: *Porta Fidei*, Para.1

Faith and Self-acceptance

I have not come to condemn the world,
but to save the world.

Jn 12: 47b

You are—in your person—an instruction, a catechism, an icon, a light to your neighbor. And in order to be all these things you have to love yourself. Love yourself, because you are called to witness the Good News, witnessing not so much through speech but through *being yourself*.

Initially it is very difficult to love ourselves. For what exactly does it mean to love oneself? The moment we ask this question we enter into the realm of faith. For without faith, we cannot love ourselves or anyone else.

This faith was given to us by baptism; and throughout our life we must grow in it. And we grow in it by praying to the Most Holy Trinity, beseeching them to give us an increase in faith. God is our Father, from whom our faith stems. Jesus Christ is our brother who brings us that faith through his life, death, and resurrection. And the Spirit is given to us by the Father just for that—to help us grow constantly in faith.

There is God and there is myself, and the two mysteries meet—God and man. Now this is what it is all about, this loving of oneself.

The wind blows where it will, says Jesus, and nobody knows where it comes from. So it is with the soul or heart. If we love, the Wind, the Holy Spirit, will take us wherever he goes, and the one who holds such a fantastic fire will teach us to begin to love ourselves as God wants us to love ourselves. Factually, what we are going to do is to love God in us.

As we begin to love ourselves, we will understand why we are loveable: we will begin to see how beautifully we are created and how lovingly. And as we think of that, we will touch God again. We will love ourselves because we constantly will see God in ourselves. Christ died to make us like God, and all this will come to us ever more clearly if we continue to beseech the most Holy Trinity for growth in faith.

But we don't know ourselves and don't love ourselves, for we don't believe in the mystery of ourselves. And that leads us inevitably to lose part of our faith, all of it.

No matter what happens to our family, what type of lifestyle we might have to change, what dangers beset us, we must begin to love ourselves. Yes, we must work toward this, and this is a tremendous work! It is almost staggering to think that one has to engage in it. Yet, it is a strange thing, for if I begin to love myself, if I begin to turn inward and look at myself—not psychiatrically speaking, not intellectually speaking, but spiritually speaking—if I turn inward and look at myself, at that very same moment I have already turned outward and loved somebody else!

Because I believe in God I believe in me, for God is in me. And once I believe in me and trust God and myself, then I can believe in everybody and trust everybody. The roots of my love for my neighbor, and for the trusting of the untrustworthy, lies in my love for myself and a trust in myself. It is a long road to travel.

Direct your attention to two points: attention to your person and attention to other persons. Unless you give attention to yourself, lovingly, with the deep realization of who you are, who made you, of your mystery and of that mystery contacting the mystery of God, you will not be able to contact and love, in a personalized way, your neighbor.

I repeat, what I am talking about isn't a psychological analysis of who we are, nor is it an attempt to discover our own identity. Far from it. What loving ourselves really means is that we become a little more quiet about our guilt and our shame. Our mind and our heart simply sink to where God is, and we begin to understand gradually how much he loves us. That is who we are. If you ask me who I am, I would answer, "I am a person beloved by God".

But coming back to faith. I am talking about that fantastic faith that means being in love with God, and really seeing God in every person, including oneself. This faith holds you and never lets you go. Faith in which you cry out to God, "Teach me to grow in faith more and more so that I may love you more and more. And so that I may love, more and more, those whom you love."

Show Your Faith

*"Do not be afraid to speak out,
nor allow yourself to be silenced:
I am with you."*

Acts 18:9

It seems today that young people are in despair. So many have a negative approach to life. Many commit suicide. Why? Because there is a lack of faith.

Somehow, we have allowed those in youth, and middle age and old age, to lose their faith. How does this happen? It happens because we do not practice it ourselves. When you see somebody practice their faith, you come and touch them. You want to be like them. You are interested.

Often those of us who have faith don't show it. We don't want to proclaim loud and clear, "I believe in God."

One day I was sitting on the subway reading a detective story and the lady next to me asked me quite directly, "Do you believe in God?" I said, "Yes, I do, thoroughly." She said, "Do you tell other people that you believe in God?" I said, "Of course I do." "Oh," she said, "so few people do."

People hunger for God as they never hungered before. They hunger for belief in him, but cannot come to this belief if no one shows them how to love God.

Let us examine our conscience very thoroughly because this is not something you write off and say is not important. It is the most important thing in our life. How do we act toward God? Do we really believe in him and take pride in acknowledging him? Or do we hide our belief away?

This is something to really pray about. Can anybody see the light of Christ through our eyes? Through our speech? Through our behavior? Do we wish to remain in darkness, and, by doing so, keep others in darkness, too?

When I pass a Catholic church I make the sign of the cross because I believe that the Blessed Sacrament is there. This lets everyone know I am a Catholic. I do it very often. It is a simple way of proclaiming my faith. In the past, even children knew that they should bless themselves in front of a church. It is something people don't think about doing, but we need to think about it.

Lately I am afraid for us Christians. It is as if we are being called to make a last stand, to proclaim the Good News that God has come on earth, that he was born, that he died, and that he resurrected—that he is our Savior. That proclamation today cannot be done only by words. It must be done is by living it.

These days terrible events are taking place in the world. They are even more terrible when they happen to people who do not believe. We have to show our belief now, because so many people will not believe in God if we don't. We have to show the face of Christ. We must be very definite. Think about the power we have to revive the faith of a soul or to kill it. What a terrible responsibility it is.

Yes, it is by touching someone who lives by the laws of Jesus Christ that men and women gather faith.

Faith in a Child

There is a child born for us,
a son given to us ...
and this is the name they give him:
Wonder-Counselor, Mighty God,
Eternal Father, Prince of Peace.

Is 9:5-6

Each year we ought to celebrate the coming of Christ with a gallant faith. It should be a faith that stands up against the whole hellish world that surrounds us today.

I know that Our Lord was born in a hell: the Romans occupied his homeland and there was great injustice. Yet, as I meditated on this, an immense peace came upon me. I want to share this peace with you.

The birth of Christ is like a gentle call. In the midst of this infinite tragedy that is the world today—its pollution, its killings—there is one consoling thing: the cry of a Child. This cry rises higher and higher than any noise of battles, any noise of cities. It rises higher than any noise and turmoil that we carry within ourselves.

It is that kind of cry that brings peace. It seems strange that a little Child can give so much peace. If you meditate on his coming you realize it is because this Child is God himself.

I came to understand a little better what faith is. From this faith in a little Child stems an inner peace that quiets the very essence of our beings whenever we feel rebellious, when we want to ask questions about these paradoxes that fill the Gospel and our lives. Very slowly, the cry of a Child begins to be the cooing of a Child. Hope is born in a manger. Above all, love, the immense fruit of faith, covers the earth.

A Living Faith

"Faith without works is dead."

cf. James 2:17

We remember what the scriptures say. Well, if faith is dead without works, then naturally we want to practice the works of mercy for our salvation. But unless there be a tremendous love, an immense delicacy, a tact beyond computing, and the ingenuity of love that turns its imagination to delicate ways of serving those in need, we will not make great dents in helping them. Love is austere. It is a two-edged sword and it can cut fine.

We run a soup kitchen. Our friend Murphy, for example, is a ne'er-do-well. He is a lousey, dirty, stinking hobo knocking at the door of Marian Center. There is nothing attractive about Murphy. In fact, everything repels you. You feel like vomiting from his stench, you detest his dirt because you are fastidious, he is a hopeless drug addict. And he is drinking himself to death. He is that kind of character. And he comes to eat! Now, why should you receive Murphy? Where does love enter into Murphy? From the will, from reason! A reason illuminated by faith that reminds us of the teaching of my Lord whom I serve, "You must love the Lord your God ... and your neighbor as yourself." (Lk 10:27-28)

Who is my neighbor? Do you remember the parable of the Samaritan? Somebody down and out, somebody up and high—all are my neighbors. And the Stranger with an Aramaic accent comes across the centuries and says, "What does it matter that you love your friends? So do the pagans. You who belong to me must love your enemies!" Then comes: "I was hungry... I was thirsty... and you never gave me anything". (cf Mt 25:31-46) Like a flash, as I behold Murphy shaking fleas and lice at my doorstep and stinking, all this passes through my head. And the gift of faith begins to act: I do believe that this man, Murphy, is Christ, and that I must love him as myself for the sake of my love of God.

My faith is at work and I act on that knowledge. I now look at Murphy with different eyes. Unless I help Murphy, I shall not fulfill the commandment to love my neighbor. These considerations are not emotional; they are intellectual and they are of faith and of grace. Love is something that comes to us from faith.

Understanding that my faith and my salvation are bound up in this character at my doorstep; seeing a rich, selfish person and yet loving him; spending yourself on a family who needs you—that is love. There is absolutely no 'liking', no emotional feelings, no success, no nothing. You do it because you love God.

Now, saints went to great degrees to make love just that—of the will directed by reason and illuminated by faith. These irrational things that come and go, such as liking or disliking are emotions. Examine yourself how through the day you live on likes and dislikes. "I don't like how he talks to me." "I don't like how he looks at me." "I don't like what she said." I, I, I, like, like, like—how can the light of love grow in all this? Unless there is a tremendous love, it is not enough. We need to implement the faith sixty seconds of every minute, sixty minutes of every hour, 24 hours a day, 365 days a year and throughout our life.

Part IV

Let us not lose sight of Jesus,
Who leads us in our faith
And brings it to perfection

Heb 12:2

In Christ, all the anguish and all the longing of the human heart finds fulfillment. The joy of love, the answer to the drama of suffering and pain, the power of forgiveness in the face of an offense received, and the victory of life over the emptiness of death: all this finds fulfillment in the mystery of His Incarnation, in His becoming man, in His sharing our human weakness so as to transform it by the power of His resurrection.

Pope Benedict XVI: *Porta Fidei*, Para. 13

A Loving Hand in Trials

Through your faith,
God's power will guard you …
even though you may for a short time
be plagued by all sorts of trials.

1Peter 1:5-6

One of the most hopeful books in the Bible is Job. His story is very simple. You remember how Satan said to God, "Look at that guy. He has everything: children, servants, flocks, good health. He has never really been tempted by miseries." So God said, "Go ahead and tempt him. I believe that he will trust in me and love me." Satan begins to tempt Job to make him give up on God. The worst things happen: all his herds and flocks are destroyed, and his children and servants have all died. Then Job himself is covered with horrible sores and ends up in the ash pit, so ugly and smelly that no one can bear to be near him. Job was absolutely down and out. And he told God how he really felt about it all. Still, he had one thing: faith! Under all kinds of difficulties he continued to believe. Now that is the yardstick of Christianity.

To believe when everything is fine, to trust when all goes well, is normal. However, to see in trials a loving hand, to believe in that fantastic mystery who is God—that takes faith. It is a strange thing, my friends. Faith shines in darkness. It comes forth under trial. It sings its song under pain.

Take my own life. I went through World War I and the revolution in Russia, and came to Canada with my husband, Boris, who was still experiencing the effects of being shell-shocked and gassed. Then our son was born. All I lived by was faith. There was nothing else to live by. I was making $7 a week. You don't go very far with a baby on $7 a week. Yet faith, like an immense tree with roots sunk deep into the underground waters of the earth, kept growing and growing within me. I could rest under the shadow of its branches. No matter how I was pushed around, I could rest. That is faith, and I'm not exactly a person who has enough faith. I should have more.

Faith walks simply, like a child, between the darkness of human life and the hope of what is to come. Faith is fundamentally a kind of folly, I guess, the folly that belongs to God himself.

There is joy in suffering when you understand and believe why you are suffering. To us Christians it is simple. For example, a woman in her thirties was diagnosed with cancer of the lungs. When the doctor told her the diagnosis, her face lit up like the sun and she said, "Thanks be to God. I now can offer something for my family, the world, and for everybody." She offered up her suffering, and the joy in her was something you could touch. Yet the pain was there, too.

Sometimes we cannot help complaining. However, anytime we are in physical or emotional pain and we accept it for the love of Christ and our brethren, something happens that is very mysterious. It is so deep, so high, so wide that nobody can measure it. Into that pain enters a power—the power of the Trinity. We are filled with the Father who gave his Son to pain, the Son who took pain upon himself to reconcile us with his Father, and the Holy Spirit who keeps hovering over us to remind us about the Son and the Father.

Look at the revolutions that have passed before our eyes and what people have had to suffer. Many had a fantastic faith and offered themselves for others. During World War II, Father Maximilian Kolbe told the Germans who were about to kill a man, "I will take his place if you let me. He has a family and I am a priest." So they killed him, and the other man survived. Years later, at the canonization of Father Kolbe, who was there in the first row? The man he had died for. That is faith.

Faith allows us to enter peacefully into the dark night that faces every one of us at one time or another. Faith is at peace and full of light. Faith considers that its precariousness and its finiteness are but the womb in which it abides, moving towards the plenitude and fullness of the eternity which it desires and believes in, and which revelation opens to it.

Faith brings into our lives such freedom, such love, such peace, and such joy that there are no words in any language that can explain it. You have to have it in order to know it. You have to experience it in order to understand it. Faith liberates. It liberates love and hope. If I am free to love and free to hope, what more do I want of life?

Love Your Enemies

"Lord, how often must I forgive?
as often as seven times?
Jesus answered, "Not seven, I tell you,
but seventy-seven times."

Mt 18:21-22

Lately I have been confronted by the misery and tragedy that surrounds us these days. Many innocent people die every day in terrible situations around the world. How much faith must I have to stand before this slaughter of the innocents? We have to look at it and still believe that the God we worship is real. Even more, my faith tells me I must love my enemies.

Why should I love my enemy? Most people believe we should kill our enemy, get rid of him. Why should I love him?

You see, when we come up against this kind of situation we are entering into a fantastic, incredible depth of faith. We are called to make a terrible act of faith in the midst of our modern society. Youth is destroying itself with drugs. Cities are in turmoil. The churches are nearly empty. Everything is a mess.

It is out of this mess that a little seed comes forth, somewhere, someplace. A small group here is trying to live the Gospel. Somewhere else others are trying to love one another. The little seed begins to grow. Eventually it will become a big tree: a tree of faith, hope and love, provided we believe. We have to believe. Every day we need to say to God, "I believe, help my unbelief!"

When I first began Friendship House in Harlem in the 1930s, I started hating the whites. I considered it to be a just hate. It shook me: the more I lived with the blacks in their poverty, and saw the discrimination, the more I shook. I lectured all over the U.S. about racial injustice. One priest said, "You went through the States like a sword of justice." After each talk, I felt like I had spent all of myself in the cause of the black people.

At that time, you couldn't imagine people in a worse situation than those who lived in Harlem. Humanly speaking I should have been a heroine, travelling around, being one of the few Catholic voices speaking about interracial justice. However, for the first year I wasn't any voice at all. The Lord was deaf to my voice because I hated the whites.

Then one day I began a retreat. I went into the church and prostrated myself as I usually do. Suddenly I saw that everything I had done was wasted because I hated the whites, hated them with a passion. I had not fulfilled what the Russians consider to be one of the great commandments of the Lord: I had not loved my enemy. In my heart, I was not at all ready to lay down my life for any white person. I wept and wept. I wept because I had alienated myself from God. I had not loved at all.

After my retreat I began talking to white people. We began to have dialogues. As time went on, changes started to happen. They happened because I was no longer alienated from God by my hatred. At Friendship House, we loved both the white and the black. It was not a superficial thing that happened overnight. It was a question of faith and of depth. We worked at it and prayed for it.

You have to love your enemy no matter who he is or how you feel. The only way it can be done is through faith.

You see, faith removes from your eyes the veil that was before them. Now you constantly see a figure on a cross who died for his enemies, and hear him say, "Father, for-

give them, for they know not what they do"
(Jn 23:34).

The Ordinary is Sacred

*The life and death of each of us
has its influence on others.*

Rom 14:7

I feel very deeply that the Lord is giving us an increased gift of faith because he knows that we need it. Yes, an increased gift of faith. This gift holds so much of God's mystery. It is of this "mystery" that I want to talk to you.

When I say faith, I mean a land of darkness and a land of pain, in a manner of speaking. For it is not easy to walk in darkness wondering about the abysses and crevices and pitfalls that might be wide open at our feet! It is not easy to walk in faith, in total belief in the Trinity: in the love of the Father; in the sustaining, warm and divine love of the Son; and the strange, incredible love of the Holy Spirit who is both Wind and Fire. It is not easy when we see the trembling of the Church, which at times seems to be poised over earthquakes. But this is the only way that is open to us. God will give us that faith, and we have to continue to pray for it so that, full of hope, we might love.

So many of us desire to console the world, to ease its pain, to do something to help it. I suggest humbly and simply, let us begin by paying attention to "our own". There are so many lonely people amongst us. Let us drop the barriers of fear, rejection, and so forth, and let us cross the divide and offer ourselves to others in our own family. There are so many lonely ones in our midst—let us go toward them, let us reduce their loneliness with the warmth of our faith, our hope, and our love. Only then can we console the rest of the world.

Our daily work—ordinary, exciting or unexciting, monotonous or un-monotonous, routine or non-routine—is, in itself, part and parcel of that faith that I talk about, that hope, that love. This workaday world of ours is the outer shell of a deep inner grace that God gives us. It is because we believe, we hope, and we love that we can do the things we can do.

Most of us still evaluate life by results, or by what we think has been achieved. Achieved in what you might call the social justice or the spiritual realm—the things that newspapers and magazines, both Christian and non-Christian, talk about. We think the routine of everyday isn't enough; we need other "important" things added.

Stop here. Please stop. Fall on your knees, pray, and listen. The darkness of faith, the walking slowly—only because we believe in the Trinity, because we hope and because we love—that, my friends, is the essence of Christianity. That is the heart of the Church; the rest flows from it. But this is to come first.

Strange as it may seem, it is the fruit of that faith and hope and love that the Lord bends over and picks up, picks up and changes the world, and allows his Church to expand because one, two, three or more people believe, hope and love.

I know the sacredness and "sacrament" of the ordinary day. I use the word "sacrament" because each day is a sacrament. Each day is a mystery. We are walking in a fantastic mystery. Don't try to figure it out. Just open your heart so that the mystery of God will meet the mystery of you. And somewhere, the two mysteries will blend. When you allow that to happen, you have peace, a fantastic peace that no one can take away from you.

The Keys of Faith

*"The mysteries of the kingdom of heaven
are revealed to you."*

Matt 13:11

Deep in the heart of faith—which is a gift
from the heart of God—lies this fantastic
understanding of who we are. This aware-
ness is transmitted to us through the sacraments that God has given us. The sacraments
sing of this faith. Each sacrament calls us to
love, each sacrament calls us to hope, and
each sacrament calls us to serve. These are
the keys faith gives us. The keys of the sacraments.

Let's reflect on the sacrament of Baptism.
Look at people who have just been baptized.
Can you see the glory within them? All their
sins are forgiven. They enter into the death
of Christ when they enter into the strange,
dark, holy waters that he himself once entered. These waters could be a sea, they
could be little lapping waves on the sand,
they could be any kind of water. All waters
became holy after he entered them.

God the Father baptizes us and his Son is
next to us, bringing to mind his own baptism. The crimson dove, the Holy Spirit, hov-

ers over us. We enter the holy of holies, the holy Catholic Church. That is, factually, the beginning and the end of faith. A baptized newborn who dies minutes later is like a star shining in the heavens of the Lord, and goes directly into his heart.

I bow low before the sacrament of the most holy Eucharist. Faith will give you the key to this sacrament, too. Try to understand it, try to understand what is not understandable. A piece of bread, a cup of wine, the ordinary things of human life for generations upon generations. That is what people ate and drank around the world. Then Our Lord took a piece of bread in his hands. He broke it and he said, "Take this, all of you, and eat it. This is my body which will be given up for you." And he raised the cup. "Take this, all of you, and drink from it. This is the cup of my blood, the blood of the new and everlasting covenant. It will poured out for many so that sins may be forgiven. Do this is memory of me" (cf. Mt 26:26-28).

Do you realize that because you believe and I believe we can move toward an altar to receive the Eucharist? It makes no difference what kind of an altar it is. It might be a stone, it might be the bed of a Nazi prisoner. It makes no difference. A man who is a priest takes a piece of bread, takes a little bit of wine, and lo and behold, faith sings a song that you can hear. You eat and drink and you have enough courage now for the next twenty-four hours to face anything and to stand firm against all that is not true or right or good.

Man sins. And Christ came to restore sinners. He became the one who took upon his shoulders all our sins, from the beginning of time to the end of the world. We are the beloved, his beloved, the ones he rescued from sin. Being the weak vessels that we are, we fall along the narrow road. Temptations, like boulders, are strewn along the path. So we come back to Christ again. We say to him, "Lord, kiss our sins away." And that is what the sacrament of Penance, confession is—the kiss of Christ. Now we are able to hear the Lord say, "Your faith has made you whole" (Lk 8:48).

Faith grows in you and me. The Church helps us along the road by giving us the beautiful sacrament of Confirmation. What does it confirm? It confirms the gift of God, confirms our faith. It makes our faith strong and immovable. Yes, it is a confirmation of depths unplumbed and mysteries unknown and yet familiar to us all. Now, hope, love, and all the seven gifts of the Holy Spirit follow.

There are other sacraments that lie in your hands: Matrimony, Holy Orders, Anointing of the Sick. As you look at your hands with the keys to the sacraments, they all suddenly change. You can hear the voice of God speaking to your heart. When he is there, love is there. When he is there, faith is there.

Now it is up to us to grow in our love and belief in him. Through our Baptism and all the sacraments, we will grow into an immense tree of faith so that people who are tired and heavy of heart will have a place to come and rest under.

Jesus Is Here

Make your home in me,
as I make mine in you.

Jn 15: 4a

I knew a little boy, Jimmy, who died at the age of fourteen. I saw him just two weeks before his death. I think of his simplicity. He said to his parents, "Oh, I have to go see my Father. My real Father who begot me. God the Father." Then, before he died he said, "Jesus is here! Jesus is here!"

That is the kind of faith we need to have: faith that is deep, profound, unsinkable, unbreakable. It is a faith that surmounts everything. It is a faith that really loves everything and everybody. Think about it.

Many nights when I'm alone I say a little prayer or two and I ask God that we would all have that faith, that simplicity of faith, that directness, just like little Jimmy. "Jesus is here. Jesus is here." That is exactly what happens. Close your eyes for a second, open them and Jesus *is* here. Jesus is in each one of you. Jesus has come in a big way. What joy that is. Yes, close your eyes, open them and say, "Jesus is here."

Fiat — Yes

The angel said to her,
"You are to conceive and bear a son,
and you must name him Jesus." ...
Mary said to the angel,
"But how can this come about,
since I am a virgin?"
..."Nothing is impossible to God."

Lk 1:30-37

Our faith—how deep, how wide is it? I think that our f-a-t-e depends on our f-a-i-t-h, because there is so little drive to practice faith. Faith may sometimes be all we have. But that means we have God. And all things are possible to God.

I keep going back to Our Lady. When the angel told Mary about her becoming the Mother of God, she said, "yes". Her *fiat* is a booming "yes," so big that we still talk about it. It carried God's reverberations. What struck me is her complete natural and supernatural acceptance of God's will. She realized fully well, in the Jewish context of that era, what it meant to be pregnant when you weren't married. What faith did it take to do that?

My attitude to Our Lady is one of awe and love. And—because she's a human being like you and I, she wasn't God—I say to my-self "What faith!" Have I got that kind of faith? I think I have faith, but then I look at her and say to myself, why don't I pray for more faith? Lord, I believe, help my unbelief.

People are beginning to go back to Our Lady. The essence is faith: that strange, incred-ible, unbelievable faith of a young girl. Faith that gave us God, God in the shape of man. Because all she would have had to say was "no".

Do I say *fiat*, "yes", to God? Think more on Mary.

When he was preaching in the Temple at 12 years of age, and Jesus said: "Don't you know? I am about my Father's business." She didn't understand that, but she said *fiat*.

After a while, her Son left her and became a preacher. Here he was going around bare-footed, preaching what appeared to be a revolutionary doctrine. She said *fiat* to it all. When things happen to us that we do not quite understand, how many times do we say "Fiat"?

When she came to see him, in front of every-body he said, "Who is my Mother? ...Any-one who does the will of my Father in heav-

en, he is my brother and sister and mother."
(Mt 12:48-50) Now, we who tremble when
anybody rejects us, who seek the approval
of our peers, we who are conformist to the
last degree—how would we take this rejection from our son? With great faith? She did;
she simply departed. Once more, she said
yes, *fiat*.

Why is it that we are unable to say "Fiat"
again and again? We go into our little cell
and hide ourselves; we think, "God doesn't
ask this of me." We need to remember that
God is first, my neighbor is second, and I am
third, and that we are called to be servants.

What is it that stops us from being who we
are, Christians, followers of Christ? We're
shy about our faith. Yet our faith is not something we "keep", it is something that we pass
on to others.

We need to turn to Our Lady in humility and
say to her, "Look, you are one of us. Teach
us the heights to which we can rise. We can't
bear Christ, but we can be "pregnant" with
love of every human being, with a never-
ceasing pregnancy, giving life to other people. Mother, teach us how to do it. Teach us
how to love. Teach us how to hope. Teach us
how to say yes to the impossible in faith."

A woman wrapped in silence, who lives in the Holy Spirit, in God the Father and God the Son. If you really don't know what to do or where to go, turn to her and she will tell you. In her awesome silence, she will solve your problem. She will, with a mother's love, a sister's love, show you the way, because she has walked it all her life—the way of her Son.

Like Mary, we should say "yes" to anything and everything that God gives us, even if it is painful. Such a small little word—*yes*—but when you say it, you become free.

Martyrdom and Death

Anyone who loses his life for my sake,
and for the sake of the Gospel,
will save it."

Mk 8:35

Do you realize that faith must be strong, stronger than death, strong as love? It stands immovable, battered by the winds of empires falling and empires rising, battered by the end of times and times to come. It makes no difference. Faith is there—strange, direct, lifting its eyes to God, unafraid.

You say that it's hard. I say, was the cross of Christ easy? Was it not made of green wood? Was the crucifixion easy? No, nothing of this was easy. Faith is possible only through love. Those who pass through pain in faith receive from God the keys of his kingdom: peace, joy, and love.

A group of Lithuanians were incarcerated in one of the gulags, the concentration camps in the Soviet Union, where many people died. One of the most beautiful things about those few Lithuanians was the rosary they made out of bread. Did you know that you can make bread into beads? Another one of the prisoners had a little Gospel. So in the night they were able to pray and recite the rosary. The faith of these people was unshakable. Then one day the guards came, took them away and shot them. Later someone found the rosary and the little Gospel and sent them to the Holy Father. They are some of his most treasured possessions.

Men cannot resist faith even when they deny it and laugh at it and jeer at it, and even kill the one who has faith. Killing those who believe is simply multiplying belief, for the blood of martyrs is the seed of faith.

Today the death of martyrs continues. Around the world women and children, young and old, are the innocent victims of bombs and bullets. In many countries priests, nuns, and lay people are still laying down their lives. They do not complain. Each one goes to their death as peacefully as a child dying in the arms of its mother. For when death is face to face with you and looks into your eyes, you reach the moment of triumph. It is probably a small moment. But it is certainly a joyous moment.

Have you ever stopped to think about death? What is it, exactly? It's a door, that's all! It is the door between this life and the next. It opens and closes, opens and closes. What does it open onto? It opens onto life, because death has been conquered long ago. This poor little moment which we call death is the door that lets us enter into life. It's nothing to be afraid of. It lets us go into the real life that we are expecting all through our earthly life. That's faith.

Other Books by Catherine Doherty

Available through Madonna House Publications

Apostolic Farming
Beginning Again
Bogoroditza: She Who Gave Birth to God
Dear Father
Dear Seminarian
Dearly Beloved: *Letters to the Children of My Spirit (3 Vol.)*
Donkey Bells: Advent and Christmas
Fragments of My Life
God in the Nitty-Gritty Life
Grace in Every Season
In the Footprints of Loneliness
In the Furnace of Doubts
Light in the Darkness
Living the Gospel Without Compromise
Molchanie: The Silence of God
Moments of Grace (perpetual calendar)
My Russian Yesterdays
Not Without Parables: *Stories of Yesterday, Today and Eternity*
On the Cross of Rejection
Our Lady's Unknown Mysteries
People of the Towel and Water, The
Poustinia: *Encountering God in Silence, Solitude and Prayer*
Season of Mercy: Lent and Easter
Sobornost: *Unity of Mind, Heart and Soul*
Soul of My Soul: Coming to the Heart of Prayer
Stations of the Cross
Strannik: The Call to the Pilgrimage of the Heart
Uródivoi: Holy Fools

Some books available in electronic format at

www.madonnahouse.org/publications